BEST WISHES

THE CAPTIVE MARINE AQUARIUM

A Colorful Photographic Resource for the Aquarist

Wayne Shang

Cover: Author's reef aquarium.

Published by Ulyssian Publications, an imprint of Pine Orchard Inc.

Visit us on the internet at www.pineorchard.com

Printed in Taiwan.

ISBN 1-930580-69-X

Library of Congress Control Number: 2004095038

To my loving wife for her endless support,

my sister for her encouragement of this book,

and

my parents who are always there for me.

Contents

Foreword

The Power of One Person

This book represents what one person, one determined person — no, what one dedicated person can do. When it comes to incredibly beautiful aquaria full of big healthy fish and fantastic corals of all shapes and sizes, one might naturally think of public aquaria which are thousands or tens of thousands of gallons in size, located in huge buildings and staffed by several professional full-time aquarists backed by a water quality laboratory. Here in these pages is the proof that those features are not required to achieve the pinnacle of success with marine aquaria.

When I first saw Wayne Shang's tanks, I couldn't believe them. The fish-only tank had the largest specimens of marine tropical fish I had ever seen in a home aquarium. Their fitness and size were better and larger, respectively, than any I had ever seen, even in a public aquarium. Plus, these were not the fish considered to be easy by the many experts in the hobby; they were difficult and impossible ones. Here they were in sizes that one can't comprehend, but you see them with your own eyes. I thought it could not be possible to surpass this accomplishment; but then, he showed me his reef tank.

Again, this tank would have been impossible to fathom, had it not been in front of my own eyes. The density, size, and variety of corals; the numbers, types, and colors of fish rivaled anything I had seen diving in places like Fiji, Bonaire, the Philippines, and Grand Cayman. The reef tank truly represented the closest I had ever seen of someone, anyone, replicating a slice of Mother Nature.

As you look through these pages, remember these are home aquaria. Their size, their location, their filtration and lighting set-ups are not complicated systems designed by some NASA-like engineering firm and professional architect. No, the components are available to anyone. The tanks and the areas around the tanks were clean and would be acceptable to any "significant other." None of the tangled cords, salt creep, smells, and assorted clutter normally associated with aquaria was present. These are pristine, beautiful showpieces that demonstrate what an "amateur" can do. Amateur in only that one is not monetarily compensated for the effort. However, there is nothing amateur about the tanks, the set-ups, the organisms, the filtration, and the results of Wayne's efforts.

Nonetheless, there is a secret ingredient. The secret ingredient that provides Wayne Shang success in my opinion? Dedication. It is obvious he is not satisfied with average, not satisfied with unsupported answers and claims, not satisfied with normal. Yes, many things are unknown about what it takes to achieve true success in this hobby. However, as this book so clearly demonstrates, one person with the will, the inquisitiveness, and the dedication to a goal can achieve the aspiration that so many strive to attain: marine aquaria that replicate and honor nature.

Enjoy this book and what it represents. In these days of "crowd following" and passive acceptance of inferior products, it is refreshing to know there are still concrete, visible examples of what one person can accomplish when he dedicates himself to a task. No committees, no big groups, no panel of experts — just a single person with a goal who builds and maintains the best closed marine aquaria possible, and provides the fish and corals the opportunity to grow and prosper as never before in captivity. It can be done. Here is the proof.

It was with pleasure that I accepted Wayne's invitation to write this foreword. Please take time to study these photos and appreciate the work, time, and dedication that is behind the results you see in these pages: they show the power of one person.

Dr. Timothy A. Hovanec

Preface

During the past two decades, the reef aquarium hobby has experienced great development. From a simple pastime, it has become a serious tool of research and a great means of observing natural behaviour to an extent where it cannot be done during a dive. A scuba dive in a coral reef can hardly be more than a short visit in another world — in the world of marine creatures, where we humans can only be a guest. But the reef aquarium gives us the opportunity to make a miniature reef grow in our living room and observe many secrets of reef life in detail. And the coral propagation techniques of aquarists are now even being employed for reef rehabilitation purposes. What greater reward could reefkeepers reap from their work!

This book authored by an ambitious reefkeeper gives an impression about how the marine aquarium hobby can be carried out. It does not attempt to present the "one and only way to a successful reef tank" as many hobbyists may do plenty things different and be successful as well. It presents Wayne's way of doing things. It depicts the methods of a successful hobbyist and of the philosophy behind his activities. But it does more than that. It also pictures the development of his aquarium over a long period of time. This teaches us an important lesson: in the reef aquarium hobby, as in life, the only constant thing is change. The reef life is dynamic. No future day will look like today nor even like this very minute.

This also applies to the aquarist. With growing knowledge and experience, our understanding of the challenges constantly evolves. Whatever we observe in our reef tank, we gain knowledge from it about aquarium techniques and about the reef life. Consequently, we aquarists have our own "dynamics" in the way we carry out this hobby; and books, like this one, help us benefit from another person's experience. Therefore, I am sure that this book with all its marine beauty and lessons of reefkeeping skills will greatly contribute to the reef aquarium hobby.

Daniel Knop
Sinsheim and Manila; January 15, 2004

Acknowledgment

My sincere thanks to Gregory McConnell; Fred Prahl; and of course, Dr. Timothy Hovanec; and Daniel Knop. This book would not have been possible without all your help.

Introduction

It all started when I was a small child. My uncle had a beach house. I used to spend the entire summer vacation playing around the seashore — boating, swimming, fishing, and snorkeling until school opened. I could not wait to go back there to do it all again the next summer. I love the ocean!

I have kept fresh water fish ever since, but never had the opportunity to own a marine aquarium. Every time I walk into an aquarium store and see the brilliant colors of the marine fish and corals, it really brings back memories of my childhood.

In the early 1980's, I started my first marine aquarium. My early efforts were not terribly successful, because I did not understand how much time and energy it would take to maintain a marine aquarium. Algae bloomed and fish died. In addition to my inexperience, information and resources were very limited at that time. But I realized that the marine life we were keeping in captivity had actually been removed from their natural environment. It is a big responsibility for us as marine aquarists to provide them with the optimum living condition to live and thrive.

Now, twenty years have passed, advanced technology and modern equipment keep being introduced into the marine aquarium hobby. We have seen increasing numbers of marine fish, corals, and invertebrates being successfully maintained and cultured in captivity, including many that were previously considered impossible to keep alive. Of course, there is still much to be studied and learned. Especially in recent years, this hobby has been justifiably criticized by environmentalists for the destruction of coral reefs.

Fortunately, today there are many commercial aquaculture facilities and breeding programs throughout the world that raise marine fish, corals, clams, and other marine life for the aquarium hobby. This significantly reduces the need for the collection of species in the wild. During the past several years, I have personally raised and given away to other aquarists large numbers of soft and stony coral fragments — enough to start many new aquariums.

This is not another how-to book for keeping marine life in captive systems. There are already many excellent books available for both amateur and advanced aquarists. Rather this book contains my reflections upon the time and effort I have devoted to the marine aquarium hobby over the past decades. I want to share my personal experience with all of you who are interested and involved in this hobby. In this book, you will discover how my system is set up, the equipment I use, and how the system is maintained. You will also have the opportunity to see many colorful pictures that are available to the public for the first time. Every single photo in this book is taken from my home aquariums, except those taken at the overseas breeding farms.

In the summer of 2001, California experienced the so-called "Energy Crisis." The dramatic increase in the cost of energy has made privately maintained marine aquariums in large scale much more difficult to own. But to me, the marine aquarium is a hobby for life. I will certainly continue to share my experience and expertise with fellow aquarists to help develop this hobby any way I can and so would you.

Enjoy!

Wayne Shang

Marine Fish Aquarium

In recent years, fish-only marine aquariums have experienced a drop in popularity. Many marine aquarists have shifted their focus to reef aquariums for their own beauty and diverse set of challenges.

Even so, a well-designed marine fish-only aquarium can be as beautiful as a reef aquarium, especially with the greatly desired colorful angel and butterfly fishes which are nearly impossible to keep in a reef aquarium as they are known to feed on coral.

In my own 300-gallon fish-only system, I have been able to keep fourteen large and three small angelfish for up to ten years. Two butterflies and two cleaner wrasses have also been in the tank for over five years.

What makes this tank so interesting is that it solely relies on live rock and sand for biological filtration. It does not utilize any type of external filtration except a large protein skimmer that keeps the nutrient level in the water low.

The large pieces of live rocks not only serve as filters; they are also purposely arranged in such a way that they break the tank into several sections which allows some particularly aggressive fish to establish their own territories.

Fish have been introduced into this tank at different times. Some of the older and more aggressive fish have to be temporarily removed in order to allow new fish a chance to settle in.

Although I have made this happen, do not think an aquarium like this is easy to accomplish. They take a great deal of time and care. For example, every time you need to remove a fish from this tank, you also have to remove almost every single piece of rock — a task I have done numerous times!

A well-managed marine fish aquarium is so relaxing to watch that one can easily fall asleep lounging on the couch.

List of the Fish	Years in Captivity
Goldflake angel (*Apolemichthys xanthopunctatus*)	9
Griffis angel (*Apolemichthys griffisi*)	8
Xanthotis angel (*Apolemichthys xanthotis*)	8
Emperor angel (*Pomacanthus imperator*)	9
Blue Line angel (*Chaetodontoplus septentrionalis*)	5
Queen angel (*Holacanthus ciliaris*)	6
Majestic angel (*Euxiphipops navarchus*)	6
Asfur angel (*Arusetta asfur*)	7
Maculosus angel (*Pomacanthus maculosus*)	7
French angel (*Pomacanthus paru*)	5
Scribbled angel (*Chaetodontoplus duboulayi*)	6
Personifer angel (*Chaetodontoplus personifer*)	6
Conspicillatus angel (*Chaetodontoplus conspicillatus*)	5
Golden angel (*Centropyge aurantius*)	7
Coral Beauty angel (*Centropyge bispinosus*)	10
Flame angel (*Centropyge loriculus*)	9
Cleaner wrasse (*Labroides dimidiatus*)	5
Golden butterfly (*Chaetodon semilarvatus*)	7

Diagrammatic view of the 300-gallon fish-only system

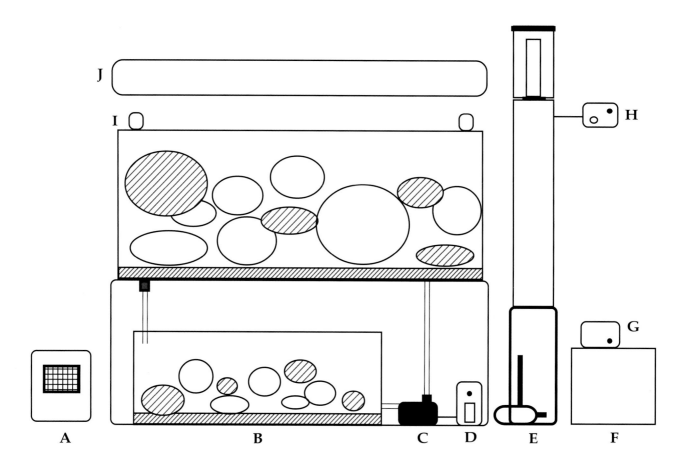

A. Teco CA680 Chiller/Heater
B. 65-gallon Sump
C. ATK 6560 centrifugal return pump
D. UPS - Uninterrupted Power Supply
E. ATK Maxi II protein skimmer
F. Freshwater reservoir
G. Freshwater doser
H. Sander 100 ozonizer
I. Tunze 2002 circulation pumps - connected to UPS
J. Lighting - Two 40-watt 50/50 and two 40-watt daylight fluorescent controlled by timer/dimmer

Water Chemistry

Specific Gravity:	1.021 ~ 1.022
Temperature:	Summer: 79 ~ 80 degrees F
	Winter: 78 ~ 79
pH:	8.2 ~ 8.3
Nitrate:	< 10 ppm (LaMotte Test Kit)
Water Change:	Approximately 25% of the water is changed every four to six weeks by either using RO/DI water mix with Instant Ocean salt or water from reef system.

Filtration

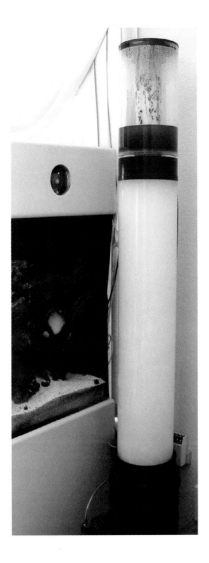

Approximately 250 pounds of live rock are inside the display tank and 175 pounds in the sump. There is also a three-inch layer of aragonite sand in both the display tank and the sump to provide additional biological filtration. No other filtration is utilized in this tank except a large size protein skimmer to keep the nutrient level low. A small amount of ozone is injected directly into the skimmer to further polish the water, also to bring up the dissolved oxygen level.

A seven-foot tall ATK skimmer.
(*above*)

Diagrammatic view of the quarantine tank

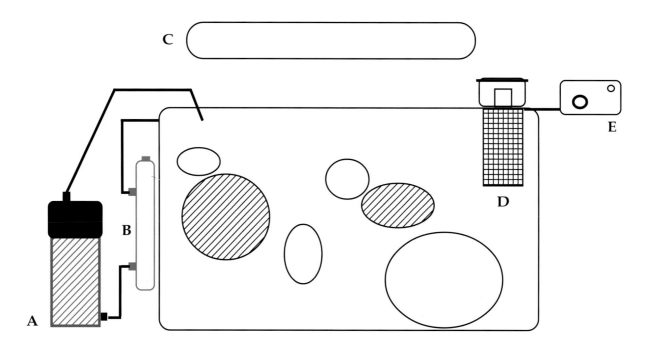

A. Eheim 2217 Canister Filter
B. 25 watt UV Sterilizer
C. 40 watt Fluorescent Light
D. Tunze 3130 Protein Skimmer
E. Sander 25mg/hr Ozonizer

Health/Disease

Newly acquired fish are kept in this 80-gallon quarantine tank (diagram shown on opposite page) for at least three weeks. The fish will be introduced into the display tank only if they are feeding aggressively and show no sign of disease.

Some aquarists achieve good results from copper-based medications, but they are not suitable for systems utilizing live rocks and sand as filtration.

A mated pair of Scribbled angels *(Chaetodontoplus duboulayi)* has been successfully kept in captivity for over six years. The larger one on top with horizontal lines on its body is the male.

Feeding/Diet

Most marine fish caught in the wild can be initially difficult to feed. Therefore, the quarantine process becomes so important because, during this period, they are allowed the chance to recognize and accept food readily. Live brine shrimps are a good beginning food. Most fish accept it easily. Gradually, it can be switched to frozen foods like plankton and mysis. Then dry foods, such as flakes and pellets, can be added as well.

Marine fish spend a considerable amount of energy purging salt from their system. Feeding them with freshwater mysis and plankton can reduce the amount of energy they spend in this process, which provides additional proteins that improve their immunity system, enhances their coloration, and increases their growth rate.

Some believe marine fish should be fed frequently in captivity with a vegetable-based diet such as steamed or frozen romaine, spinach, and broccoli. However, this can lead to a rapid build-up of dissolved organic materials in the water. Today, the majority of commercially available dry foods contain some sort of seaweed or spirulina algae. This should provide enough fiber, vitamin A, and vitamin C to meet their dietary requirements.

The fishes in my own system are fed two or three times a day. In the morning, marine pellets are soaked in multi-vitamin solutions before feeding. An automatic feeder will drop small amount of mid-size pellets just to keep the fishes active during the day. Frozen mysis and plankton are served sometimes in the evening.

"...the number of angelfish that could be fit in an aquarium has been the subject of lively debate among saltwater enthusiasts for decades. Way

as come close to providing one unforgettable answer in a 300-gallon system that many experts would classify as an impossible or a miracle."

Michael S. Paletta

Aufur angel (*Arusetta asfur*)

❏ **Origin:** Red Sea.
❏ **Captive Behavior:** Hardy; not as aggressive as the Maculosus angel from the same region.

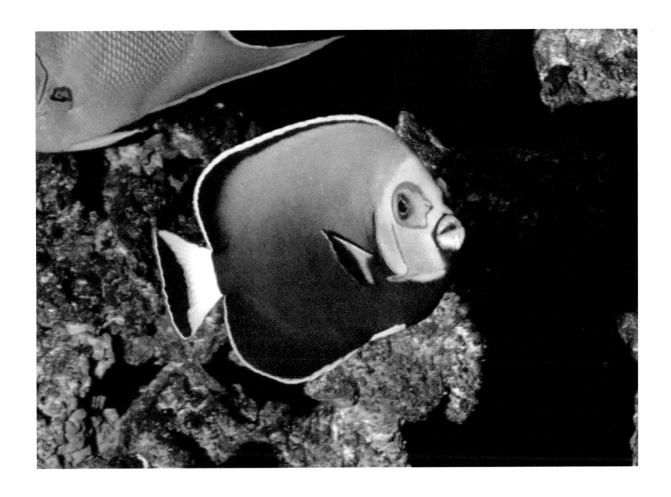

Conspicillatus angel (*Chaetodontoplus conspicillatus*)

❏ **Origin:** New Caledonia.
❏ **Captive Behavior:** Active but peaceful; an outgoing species that requires large open space.

Emperor angel (*Pomacanthus imperator*)

❏ **Origin:** Red Sea.
❏ **Captive Behavior:** Aggressive; a territorial species that requires plenty of hiding space.

French angel (*Pomacanthus paru*)

❏ **Origin:** Western Atlantic.
❏ **Captive Behavior:** Aggressive; a territorial species that requires plenty of hiding space.

Maculosus angel (*Pomacanthus maculosus*)

❏ **Origin:** Red Sea.
❏ **Captive Behavior:** Aggressive; a hardy species that can grow very fast in captivity.

Griffis angel (*Apolemichthys griffisi*)

❏ **Origin:** Western and Central Pacific.
❏ **Captive Behavior:** Active; only shows aggressiveness to members of its own *Apolemichthys* family-Xanthotis and Goldflake angels.

Goldflake angel (*Apolemichthys xanthopunctatus*)

❏ **Origin:** Oceania.
❏ **Captive Behavior:** Active; only shows aggressiveness to members of its own *Apolemichthys* family -
Xanthotis and Griffis angels.

Xanthotis angel (*Apolemichthys xanthotis*)

❏ **Origin:** Red Sea.
❏ **Captive Behavior:** Active; only shows aggressiveness to members of its own *Apolemichthys* family -
   Griffis and Goldflake angels.

Majestic angel (*Euxiphipops navarchus*)

❏ **Origin:** Western Pacific.
❏ **Captive Behavior:** Shy; difficult to feed initially; juvenile specimens adapt better to captive system.

Scribbled angel (*Chaetodontoplus duboulayi*)

❏ **Origin:** Great Barrier Reef.
❏ **Captive Behavior:** Active yet peaceful; a friendly outgoing species that can feed out of your hand.

Golden butterfly (*Chaetodon semilarvatus*)

❏ **Origin:** Red Sea.
❏ **Captive Behavior:** Shy; difficult to feed initially; very sensitive to water quality.

Reef Aquarium

Reef aquaria are considered the most beautiful and interesting among all different types of aquaria. Many people are attracted to them because of their brilliant colors and exotic appearance.

A reef aquarium is not as difficult to set up as most people may think and it does not need to be complicated.

You will soon notice that every one of my marine systems share the same simple concept. They all rely on live rock and deep sand bed for biological filtration with the addition of a powerful protein skimmer/foam fractioner to keep the nutrient level low inside the system.

The main way reef systems differs from fish-only systems is that while the reef inhabitants grow, they use specific elements for the formation of their tissues and skeletons. Regardless of whether it's major, minor, or trace element, they all need to be replenished to support the continuous growth. This can easily be accomplished by partial water changes or adding the elements back into the system. However, in order to know the exact water condition, not only do the water parameters such as temperature, salinity, and pH level need to be closely monitored; but also water testing including alkalinity, calcium, magnesium, and iodine need to be performed on a regular basis.

Diagrammatic view of the 700-gallon reef system

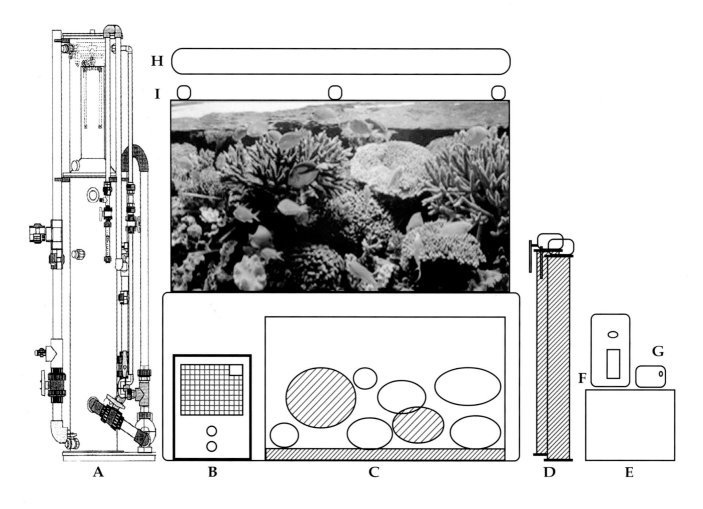

A. Sander Helgoland 300 protein skimmer
B. Teco CA 2000 Chiller/Heater
C. 200-gallon sump
D. Korallin calcium reactor
E. Freshwater/kalkwasser reservoir

F. UPS - Uninterrupted Power Supply
G. Freshwater/Kalkwasser doser
H. Lighting
I. Tunze 2002 circulation pumps -
connected to UPS

Filtration

Approximately 600 pounds of live rock are inside the 700-gallon display tank and an additional 300 pounds in the sump. There is also a three-inch layer of aragonite sand in both display tank and sump. The thick layer of sand bed not only provides additional denitrification, but also helps to maintain both the alkalinity and calcium level through the dissolution of the aragonite.

There is no other type of filtration in this system except a very large protein skimmer/foam fractioner.

A microprocessor controlled lighting system was tested on my holding tank. This advanced lighting equipment have built-in timer and moonlight that goes with the lunar cycle. However, its long-term reliability and performance are still uncertain.

Lighting

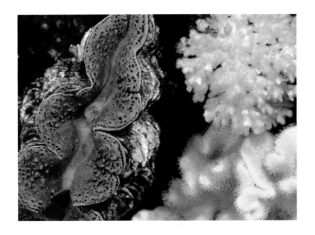

The colorful corals, clams, and invertebrates that marine aquarists like to keep in captive system are from very shallow reef areas. High intensity lights at specific wavelengths are required for photosynthesize and also to maintain coloration.

Around 1995, the 10,000 and 20,000 K (degrees Kelvin) metal halide bulbs were introduced into the marine aquarium hobby. These higher color temperature metal halides, with addition of actinic fluorescent bulbs that are widely used by marine aquarists, can provide stronger blue, green, violet, and UV-A that more closely match the type of lights that marine life receives in its natural environment.

In my own 700-gallon reef system, there are four 400-watt (14,000 K) and two 1,000-watt (10,000 K) metal halides, plus six 60-watt actinic fluorescent bulbs. The metal halides are on for 10 hours per day and the actinic are on for 14 hours. On top of these, there are two 40-watt blue halogen bulbs working as moonlight that are controlled by a lunar controller. The moonlight might have something to do with regular spawning activities of the *Tridacna* clams in my reef system.

Protein Skimmer/ Foam Fractioner

Protein skimmer/foam fractioners have been around for decades and I believed they are by far the most efficient piece of equipment in removal of nutrients from marine aquarium.

Some aquarists may argue that other forms of filtration, such as algae or mud filters, can also do wonders for marine aquaria. But, it would be more convincing to see more successful marine systems that solely rely on these types of filtration.

Moreover, today a large number of the marine systems utilize calcium reactors to keep up the demand of calcium and buffer. The effluent from the reactor is low in pH; a properly functioning protein skimmer can provide additional gas exchange to assist maintaining the pH at the right level.

A Sander Helgoland 300 protein skimmer. (*left*)
Close-up shot of the skimmer output. (*above*)

Water Circulation

Water current not only brings food to the corals, it also carries their waste products away. Most of the corals we try to keep in captive systems are from very high-energy shallow reef areas, and they require moderate to strong water motion to thrive.

Besides, corals, especially small-polyped stony coral, can release a lot of slime when distressed. Thus, adequate water movement in reef aquaria becomes important to their health.

Although it is almost impossible for us to provide the same water motion as the corals receive in their natural environment, we can still partially simulate this condition by connecting water pumps or powerheads to a timer/wave maker.

In my 700-gallon reef system, the main circulation is provided by two centrifugal pumps that each move 1,950 gallons of water per hour. They return water from the sump back to the top of the tank. Water motion is made by another two ATK pumps that are controlled by a timer/wave maker.

One ATK centrifugal circulation pump. (*top*)
Two ATK pumps controlled by a wavemaker. (*above*)

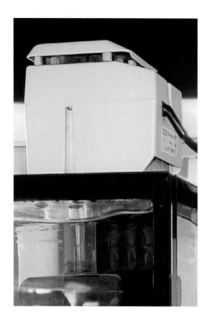

Five Tunze Turbelle external pumps are also installed to create additional water currents. All wave-making water pumps on this system are connected to an uninterrupted power supply in case of power failure. The power supply can operate these pumps for approximately four hours before the back-up power generator is started.

Tunze Turbelle pump. (*above*)
Uninterrupted Power Supply. (*right*)

Water Chemistry

Specific Gravity:	1.023 ~ 1.024
Temperature:	Summer: 78 ~ 80 degrees F
	Winter: 80 ~ 82
pH:	8.1 ~ 8.3
Alkalinity/Carbonate Hardness:	10 ~ 12 dKH (Tropic Marine Test Kit)
Calcium:	450 ppm (Lamotte/Tropic Marine Test Kit)
Magnesium:	1300 ppm (Tropic Marine Test Kit)
Iodine:	.06 ppm (Salifert Test Kit)
Nitrate:	None (LaMotte Test Kit)
Phosphate:	None (LaMotte Test Kit)
Water Change:	Approximately 10% of the water is drained directly from the fish-only system every four to six weeks just to benefit the large population of *Tridacna* Clams.

Water Temperature

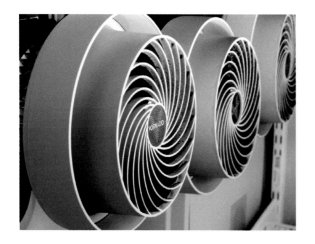

Water temperature is maintained at 78 to 80 degrees F in winter and 80 to 82 degrees F in summer. The reason it shifts a few degrees between winter and summer is just to save energy cost.

In recent years, more aquarists tend to keep the aquarium temperatures at 80 degrees F or higher. My observation is that as long as the temperature does not go beyond 82 degrees F, it will not cause any harm to the aquarium inhabitants including small polyps stony corals and clams.

Cooling fans blow across the top of the aquarium help to lower the water temperature. (*above*)
A large-size chiller was utilized to control water temperature in summer. (*right*)

An electronic monitor/controller. (*Above*)

The pH value of natural seawater ranges between 8.0 to 8.2 from region to region. In the early 80's, many books and periodicals suggest that pH values in marine systems should be at 8.3 or higher. Therefore, some test kit manufacturers tend to adjust their kits to read a little bit higher than normal. High pH value could assist in control of undesirable algae. But in a well-maintained reef aquarium, the nutrients level should be at a minimum and filamentous algae should not be a concern.

Today, large numbers of reef aquariums are equipped with a calcium reactor. The pH values in this type of system do not normally rise above 8.3 during the day and can fall below 8.0 at night. Daily fluctuation of pH range in reef aquaria in between 8.0 and 8.4 is acceptable. Good water circulation and properly sized protein skimmers can also assist in stabilizing the pH value in a closed system.

Alkalinity

Alkalinity is a measure of the concentration of carbonate and hydrogen carbonate ions in water. The alkalinity of natural seawater is around 2.5 meq/L that is approximately 7 German degrees of carbonate hardness (dKH).

In a closed system, during the bacterial decomposition of organic waste that is produced by marine life, acids are released into the water. The alkalinity level has a tendency to fall over a period of time, so buffers are required to maintained the proper level.

It is recommended that the alkalinity values in reef aquaria be maintained between 7 to 10 dKH. Studies done at one university a couple of years ago showed corals have the best growth rate when the carbonate hardness is at 12 degrees. High KH levels also help to keep pH steady in reef systems.

A hard tube worm *Serpulid* sp.
(*above*)

Calcium

In natural seawater, the concentration of calcium ($Ca2+$) ranges from 380 to 450 ppm (mg/L).

In captive reef aquaria, calcifying organisms consume calcium, magnesium, strontium, and other elements to form their hard skeletons. If the system houses dense populations of stony corals and clams, the calcium will deplete rapidly. Therefore, the calcium level must be maintained in order to keep up their calcification rate.

Three methods are most commonly used by marine aquarists to maintain the calcium and alkalinity level in their captive systems:

Two-Part Solution
(Calcium Chloride and Sodium Carbonate or Sodium Hydrogen Carbonate)

Calcium chloride can be added into aquarium water to increase the calcium concentration. However, this cannot be achieved unless the alkalinity is also within proper ranges. Carbonate buffers also need to be added at the same time.

The two solutions are prepared and stored separately, then added into the aquarium at regular intervals.

One must be aware that if a reef system is solely relying on this method to maintain its calcium and alkalinity level, the salinity of aquarium water could rise over period of time. This is because when calcium chloride and sodium carbonate are being added into the aquarium water, the sodium chloride (salt) is also formed and accumulated. Although small amounts of salt are constantly removed by the protein skimmer, the specific gravity should still be closely monitored and adjusted accordingly.

Kalkwaseer (Limewater)

Kalkwasser is a saturated solution of calcium hydroxide. It is probably the most commonly used method for calcium maintenance in reef aquaria.

In captive reef systems, adding Kalkwasser can also help to maintain the pH and alkalinity level by neutralizing acids that are created in the nitrogen cycle. In addition, it helps to precipitate phosphate from the aquarium water.

The fresh mixed Kalkwasser solution has a high pH value. To avoid pH shock to marine life, the Kalkwasser solution should be slowly dosed into the aquarium, preferably at night when the pH is low.

Calcium Reactor

Calcium reactors started to gain popularity in mid-1990's. These are a device whereby aquarium water is continuously circulated through a column filled with calcareous media while carbon dioxide (CO_2) is injected. In the process the CO_2 is consumed, pH drops and calcareous media is dissolved, resulting in a high calcium hydrogen carbonate concentration.

The advantage of using a calcium reactor is that it provides both calcium (Ca2+) and bicarbonates ions in the same ratio as they are consumed during the calcification.

To avoid undesirable elements leaching into the aquarium, such as phosphate, only pure limestone granulate or aragonite material should be used in the reactor.

Conclusion

The first two methods are best used on small to medium reef systems. Some aquarists get very good results by using kalkwasser alone or adding the required amount of the two part solutions regularly.

The calcium reactor is best suited to medium to large reef systems. Although its initial expense is high, it does offer other benefits such as low operating cost and easy maintenance.

To ensure proper growth of *Tridacna* clams in closed system, calcium concentration should be closely monitored. (*right*)

In my own reef system, owing to the high density of stony coral and large populations of *Tridacna* clams, all three methods are utilized in order to keep up with demand! The pictures on the following pages should give you a pretty good idea why it is all necessary.

Two 42-inch tall calcium reactors are operated in series. CO_2 is injected only into the first unit; the water then flows thru the second unit where the residual CO_2 is further consumed. As a result, greater dissolution of calcareous media and higher KH/calcium ions are produced. The second unit also prevents excessive CO_2 from going into the aquarium, which can cause the pH level to drop and promote filamentous algae. In addition, approximately eight gallons of Kalkwasser are dosed throughout the night. Occasionally, two-part calcium carbonate buffers are added to boost the calcium and alkalinity level.

Two large calcium reactors operated in series. (*right*)

Magnesium

Magnesium is a component of the seawater buffer system. Low magnesium concentration makes it difficult to maintain proper calcium and alkalinity level in a closed system.

In some synthetic salt mixes, the magnesium is intentionally left out in order to make it dissolve faster. These type of salt mixes are unsuitable for reef aquariums.

The magnesium concentration in natural seawater is approximately 1300 ppm. Some older reef systems might experience difficulty in keeping up the calcium and alkalinity, unless the magnesium is restored back to its ideal level.

Strontium

Strontium is an essential trace element in reef aquaria. It stimulates growth in stony corals and assists in the development of desirable coralline algae.

The strontium concentration, in my reef system, relies on the dissolution of limestone granulate in the calcium reactor. No additional strontium supplement is added into the aquarium on a regular basis, since there is no commercially available strontium test kit that is easy to use and reliable.

A red color *Goniopora* sp. (*top*)

Water Change

Water is changed every four to six weeks. Normally, the water is drained from the fish-only tank directly into reef system. If no new coral was introduced during that period of time, the water of the reef system is then pumped back into the fish-only tank. It is a kind of recycling process.

The reason that nutrient rich water is brought into the reef system from fish-only system is mainly to benefit the large population of *Tridacna* clams. Of course, other corals might also benefit from this practice.

The nitrate level in the fish-only system is normally around 10 ppm. This will bring up the nitrate level of the reef system just a little. But, it will drop back down to zero in just a couple of days.

Recycling water back and forth between the fish-only and the reef aquarium does not seem to be common. This practice requires close monitoring of the water chemistry, which means the water tests must be performed frequently. I find this is something most aquarists do not like to do.

Added benefits of this practice are conservation of fresh water and synthetic salt mix.

Above & Opposite: 300-gallon reef aquarium. (1997)

Above & Opposite: Close up shots of 300-gallon reef. (1998)

Above & Opposite: 300-gallon reef system. (1999)

Above & Opposite: Close up shots of 300-gallon reef. (1999)

Above & Opposite: 180-gallon coral-propagation/holding tank.

Above & Opposite: 700-gallon reef system.

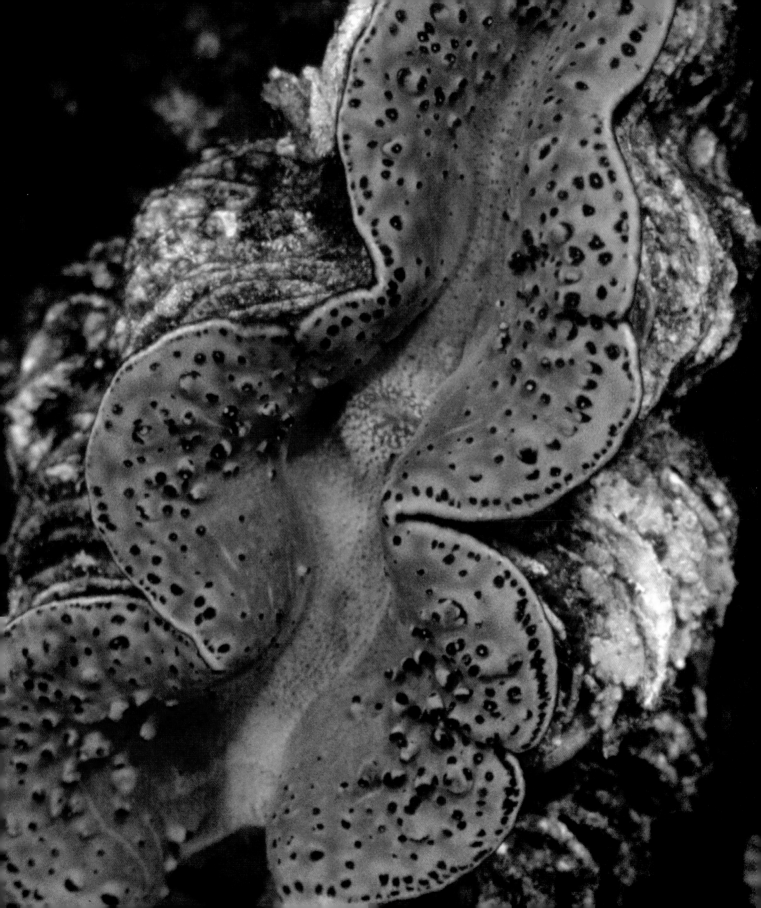

Tridacna Clams

The unique pattern and brilliant-colored mantle have made *Tridacna* clams very popular in the recent years. However, to raise them in a captive system for long periods of time is still a challenge even for some experienced aquarists.

The *Tridacna* clams are filter feeders. Their colorful mantle houses symbiotic algae (zooxanthellae). During photosynthesis, the symbiotic algae absorb nutrients from their surrounding water to produce food for the clams.

In 1995, I introduced a couple of large *Tridacna derasa* into the sump of my fish-only system as supplementary filtration to lower the nitrate level. The idea was first published in early 1997 when *Aquarium Frontier* magazine featured my marine aquariums. Over the past several years, it has been proven that every one of my systems with high population of *Tridacna* clams all show very low nutrient level. Beyond that, all corals inside the system have showed a remarkable growth rate.

This colorful *Tridacna crocea* was bred in captivity at MMDC (Micronesian Mariculture Demonstration Center) at Koror, Palau.

Captive bred *Tridacna crocea* from Palau.

Captive bred *Tridacna crocea* from Palau.

Captive bred *Tridacna crocea* from Palau.

Captive bred *Tridacna crocea* from Palau.

Captive bred *Tridacna crocea* from Palau.

Captive bred *Tridacna crocea* from Palau.

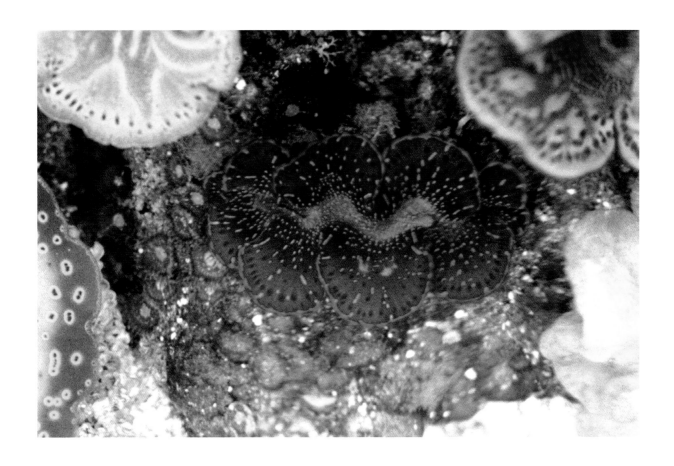

Tridacna maxima from Pohnpei.

Tridacna maxima from Pohnpei.

Tridacna maxima from Pohnpei.

Tridacna maxima from Pohnpei.

Tridacna maxima from Pohnpei.

Tridacna maxima from Pohnpei.

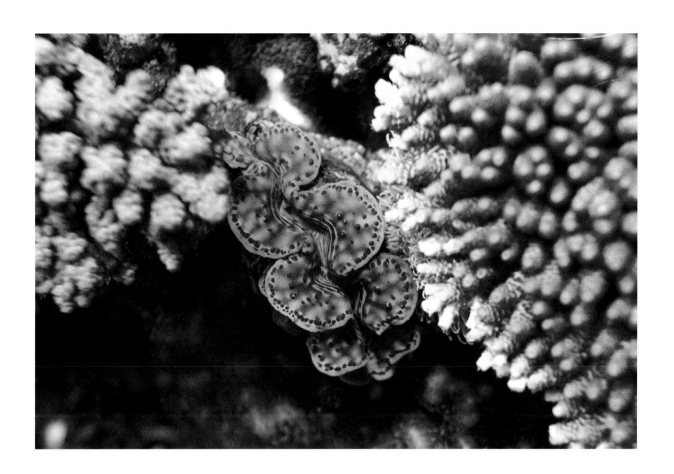

Tridacna maxima from Pohnpei.

This giant clam was shipped to me as a Red Sea *Tridacna maxima.*
I later learned there never had been a CITES (Convention on International Trade in Endangered Species) permit to export clams from the Red Sea. So I guess, they either got out by accident or maybe from elsewhere.

Red Sea *Tridacna maxima.*

Red Sea *Tridacna maxima.*

1 - *Tridacna gigas.*
2 - *Tridacna maxima.*
3 - *Tridacna crocea.*

Tridacna maxima from Red Sea (middle), *Tridacna crocea* from Paula (right).

Tridacna maxima from Pohnpei.

Tridacna maxima from Pohnpei.

Tridacna maxima from Marshall Islands.

Tridacna derasa.

Tidacna gigas.

Tridana gigas is one of the largest and fastest growing species in *Tridacna* family. This *Tidacna gigas* has been raised in captivity for more than ten years. It measures about 22 inches across, weighs approximately 40 pounds and is still growing!

During the spawning period, the water can turn cloudy quickly.

Spawning Behaviors in Captive System

Tridacna clams can spawn in captive systems and this is often caused by extreme factors such as sudden change in water or light conditions.

During the past several years, I have witnessed numerous mass spawning activities. The *Tridacna croceas, maxima, squamosa* and *gigas* have all spawned in my reef system. And it becomes a regular pattern that the mass spawning activities happen every three to four months, normally a few days after the full moon.

The spawning activities, in a closed system, provide natural food source for its inhabitants.

The ***Tridacna crocea*** (*left*) and ***Tridana maxima*** (*right*) spawn simultaneously.

A spawning *Tridacna maxima.*

A ***Tridacna maxima*** joins in the mass spawning activity.

A spawning *Tridacna squamosa*.

A spawning *Tridacna derasa*.

Reef-Building Stony Corals

A few years ago, reef building (small-polyped) stony corals were almost impossible to keep alive in a home aquarium. Steve Tyree is one of the pioneers in the United States who started to raise small-polyped stony coral in early 1990. It was a true inspiration when I first saw pictures of his small-polyped-stony-corals dominated reef aquarium!

Today, with all the modern equipment and techniques, plus the information that is easily available throught the Internet, the challenges we face are no longer just to keep these corals alive in captivity but to keep them from overgrowing in our system.

Acropora nobilis

❏ Captive Difficulty: Moderate to difficult.
❏ Lighting Requirements: Strong.
❏ Current Requirements: Moderate to strong.

Acropora yongei

❏ Captive Difficulty: Moderate.
❏ Lighting Requirements: Moderate to strong.
❏ Current Requirements: Moderate to strong.

Acropora formosa

- ❑ Captive Difficulty: Moderate.
- ❑ Lighting Requirements: Moderate to strong.
- ❑ Current Requirements: Moderate.

The tiny white spots on branches of this *Acropora formosa* look like egg/sperm. But, the spawning event has never been captured.

Pocillopora damicornis

❏ Captive Difficulty: Easy.
❏ Lighting Requirements: Moderate to strong.
❏ Current Requirements: Moderate.

Acropora millepora

❏ Captive Difficulty: Easy.
❏ Lighting Requirements: Moderate.
❏ Current Requirements: Moderate.

Seriatopora hystrix

❏ Captive Difficulty: Moderate to difficult.
❏ Lighting Requirements: Moderate to strong.
❏ Current Requirements: Moderate.

Stylophora pistillata

❏ Captive Difficulty: Easy.
❏ Lighting Requirements: Moderate to strong.
❏ Current Requirements: Moderate.

Seriatopora hystrix

Stylophora pistillata

Seriatopora hystrix

Acropora loripes

❏ Captive Difficulty: Difficult.
❏ Lighting Requirements: Moderate to strong.
❏ Current Requirements: Moderate to strong.

Acropora loripes

- ❏ Captive Difficulty: Difficult.
- ❏ Lighting Requirements: Moderate to strong.
- ❏ Current Requirements: Moderate to strong.

Acropora loripes

❑ Captive Difficulty: Difficult.
❑ Lighting Requirements: Moderate to strong.
❑ Current Requirements: Moderate to strong.

Acropora loripes

❏ Captive Difficulty: Difficult.
❏ Lighting Requirements: Moderate to strong.
❏ Current Requirements: Moderate to strong.

Acropora tenuis

❏ Captive Difficulty: Moderate to difficult.
❏ Lighting Requirements: Moderate to strong.
❏ Current Requirements: Moderate.

Acropora tenuis

❏ Captive Difficulty: Moderate to difficult.
❏ Lighting Requirements: Moderate to strong.
❏ Current Requirements: Moderate.

Acropora humilis

❏ Captive Difficulty: Moderate to difficult.
❏ Lighting Requirements: Moderate to strong.
❏ Current Requirements: Moderate.

Acropora humilis

❑ Captive Difficulty: Moderate to difficult.
❑ Lighting Requirements: Moderate to strong.
❑ Current Requirements: Moderate.

Acropora humilis

❏ Captive Difficulty: Moderate to difficult.
❏ Lighting Requirements: Moderate.
❏ Current Requirements: Moderatt to strong.

Acropora samoensis

❏ Captive Difficulty: Moderate to difficult.
❏ Lighting Requirements: Moderate to strong.
❏ Current Requirements: Moderate.

***Acropora* sp.**

(Fragment of Steve Tyree's Purple-Monster)

❑ Captive Difficulty: Difficult.
❑ Lighting Requirements: Moderate to strong.
❑ Current Requirements: Moderate to strong.

Acropora monticulosa

❏ Captive Difficulty: Difficult.
❏ Lighting Requirements: Moderate to strong.
❏ Current Requirements: Moderate.

Acropora valida

❏ Captive Difficulty: Easy.
❏ Lighting Requirements: Moderate to strong.
❏ Current Requirements: Moderate.

Acropora valida

❏ Captive Difficulty: Easy.
❏ Lighting Requirements: Moderate to strong.
❏ Current Requirements: Moderate.

Acropora bushyensis

❏ Captive Difficulty: Moderate to difficult.
❏ Lighting Requirements: Moderate to strong.
❏ Current Requirements: Moderate.

Acropora divaricata

❑ Captive Difficulty: Moderate to difficult.
❑ Lighting Requirements: Moderate to strong.
❑ Current Requirements: Moderate.

Acropora selago

❏ Captive Difficulty: Moderate to difficult.
❏ Lighting Requirements: Moderate to strong.
❏ Current Requirements: Moderate.

Acropora secale

❏ Captive Difficulty: Moderate to difficult.
❏ Lighting Requirements: Moderate to strong.
❏ Current Requirements: Moderate.

Acropora variolosa

❏ Captive Difficulty: Moderate.
❏ Lighting Requirements: Moderate to strong.
❏ Current Requirements: Moderate.

Acropora subulata

❏ Captive Difficulty: Moderate.
❏ Lighting Requirements: Moderate to strong.
❏ Current Requirements: Moderate.

Pocillopora elegans

❏ Captive Difficulty: Moderate.
❏ Lighting Requirements: Moderate to strong.
❏ Current Requirements: Moderate.

Montipora digitata

❏ Captive Difficulty: Easy.
❏ Lighting Requirements: Moderate.
❏ Current Requirements: Weak to moderate.

Acropora divaricata

❏ Captive Difficulty: Moderate to difficult.
❏ Lighting Requirements: Moderate to strong.
❏ Current Requirements: Moderate.

Acropora seriata

❏ Captive Difficulty: Moderate.
❏ Lighting Requirements: Moderate to strong.
❏ Current Requirements: Moderate.

Acropora chesterfieldensis

❏ Captive Difficulty: Easy to moderate.
❏ Lighting Requirements: Moderate to strong.
❏ Current Requirements: Moderate.

Acropora spicifera

- ❏ Captive Difficulty: Easy to moderate.
- ❏ Lighting Requirements: Moderate.
- ❏ Current Requirements: Moderate.

Acropora carduus

❏ Captive Difficulty: Moderate.
❏ Lighting Requirements: Moderate to strong.
❏ Current Requirements: Moderate.

As in their natural environment, corals compete for space in a captive reef aquarium. Two *Acropora* species were left unchecked and are starting to show damages.

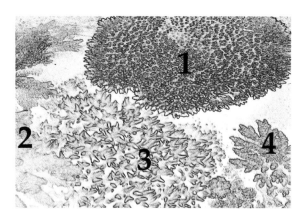

1 - *Acropora hyacinthus*
2 - *Acropora nobilis*
3 - *Seriatopora hystrix*
4 - *Acropora nasuta*

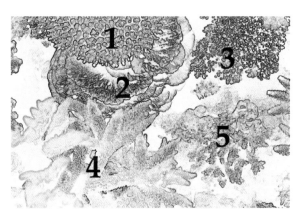

1 - *Acropora hyacinthus*
2 - *Montipora capricornis*
3 - *Acropora carduus*
4 - *Acropora formosa*
5 - *Acropora subulata*

Growth Sequence

The growth rate of reef building stony coral in captive reef aquaria varies from one species to another. The water parameters and quality of the light are the two most important factors. If optimum conditions are provided, these corals can reach almost the same growth rate as they do in their natural environment.

The photographic documentation during their growth period not only provides a record of their growth history but also shows proof that marine aquarists did not just take them from the natural reef area for enjoyment. We can also raise them in captivity!

The following pages show growth sequences of four species that were kept in captivity: *Acropora nobolis, Acropora yongei, Acropora cytherea* and *Acropora millepora.*

This true staghorn *Acropora nobilis* is considered a difficult species to keep because of its ability to produce a lot of slime when disturbed. Photo above: June 2000

1	2
3	4
5	6

Opposite - Growth sequence of ***Acropora nobilis***:

1 - July 1995 - Imported from Fiji.
2 - Feb. 1996.
3 - Jan. 1997.
4 - Summer 1997 - Damaged due to an accident (equipment failure).
5 - May 1998 - Starting to re-grow.
6 - Sep. 1999 - Developed into thicker and multiple branches.

Growth sequence of **Acropora yongei**:

1 - August 1998 - Imported from Fiji.
2 - July 1999.
3 - January 2000.
4 - June 2000.

1	2
3	4

This true staghorn *Acropora yongei* is easy to keep and grows fairly quickly in a captive system. Its fragments have been widely spread.   Photo above: July 2000.

Growth sequence of **Acropora hyacinthus**:

Top: Imported from Solomon Island in June 1999.
Above: May 2000.

This *Acropora hyacinthus* can grow into its natural tabletop shape if cared for properly in captivity. Photo above: December 2000.

1	2
3	4

Growth sequence of *Acropora millepora:*

1 - First acquired as a 3-inch fragment.
2 - 3 month.
3 - 1 year.
4 - 2 years.

This *Acropora millepora* grew from a 3-inch fragment into a 24-inch diameter colony in just about three years. In late 1999, I not only ran out of space in my 300-gallon tank but tired of trimming it every week. Steve Tyree was contacted and we decided to move it to a newly set-up reef aquarium in southern California.

"This may have been the largest Acropora ever transported over 400 land miles..."

Steve Tyree
dynamicecomorphology.com

A small fragment of the giant *millepora* that I have saved for myself.

Interestingly, under the new 14K metal halide bulbs that I received from Germany in 2001, this *Millepora* species is slowly turning blue!

Reef Fishes

Because their natural diet does not exist in a closed system, reef fishes require frequent feeding in order to survive in captivity, especially the colorful anthias that feed on zooplankton in their natural environments.

Marine aquarists struggle between providing the optimum water condition for corals to thrive and adding diverse types of fishes to create a natural-looking reef aquarium. I believe the key is finding the right balance.

The majority of fish foods contains a high level of phosphorus that can lead to the outbreak of undesirable algae in a closed system. If the system does not have an adequate protein skimmer or other forms of filtration to export excessive waste products, the nutrient level in the water will increase rapidly, unless mass water changes are performed on regular basis.

The fish featured in this section were successfully maintained in captive reef systems without causing any harm to the coral inhabitants.

The colorful anthias are a welcome addition to reef aquariums. However, keeping them in captivity for long periods of time is still quite a challenge for marine aquarists.

Pseudanthias pictili

❏ **Origin:** Australia.
❏ **Captive Behavior:** A very difficult species to acclimate. It can take as long as four weeks for them to start to accept fish food in a captive aquarium.

Pseudanthias pictilis (female)

Pseudanthias pictilis (male)

Above: **Pseudanthias bartlettorum** (female).
Left: A female is undergoing sex change.

Pseudanthias bartlettorum (male)

❏ **Origin:** Hawaii.
❏ **Captive Behavior:** An easy *Anthia* species to keep. The females tend to change their sex to male more frequently in captivity.

Pseudanthias bimaculatus (male)

❏ **Origin:** Maldives.
❏ **Captive Behavior:** A hardy species, but it can be difficult to feed when first
   introduced to captive aquariums. It's another *Anthia* species in which females
   tend to change their sex to male more frequently in captivity.

Opposite above & below:
Pseudanthias bimaculatus (female)

Above: **Pseudanthias squamipinnis** (female).
Left: A shoal of Lyretail Anthias - **Pseudanthias squamipinnis.**

Pseudanthias squamipinnis (male)

❏ **Origin:** Fiji.
❏ **Captive Behavior:** Aggressive, but a fairly easy anthias species to keep in a captive aquarium.

Mirolabrichthys bicolor

❏ **Origin:** Hawaii.
❏ **Captive Behavior:** Needs to be feed frequently; a difficult species to keep
   for a long period of time.

Serranocirrhitus latus - Sunburst anthias

❏ **Origin:** Fiji.
❏ **Captive Behavior:** Very cute but shy species.

Pseudanthias dispar

❏ **Origin:** Indian Ocean.
❏ **Captive Behavior:** Peaceful; requires frequent feeding to survive in captivity.

Opposite:
A mixed shoal of anthias and surgeons
were introduced into the 700-gallon tank
to create a natural-looking reef aquarium.

Surgeons and tangs are herbivorous fish; they help to control unwanted algae growth. This makes them well suitable for reef aquariums. However, these fishes are prone to *Amyloodinium* and *Crypotocaryon* (white spot/saltwater ich) diseases; an initial quarantine process is a must.

Zebrasoma xanthurus (Purple Tang)

❑ **Origin:** Red sea.
❑ **Captive Behavior:** Territorial. Needs plenty of algal foods to maintain their health.

Acanthurus sohal (Sohal Tang)

❏ **Origin:** Red Sea.
❏ **Captive Behavior:** Active and aggressive. Can grow very fast in captivity.

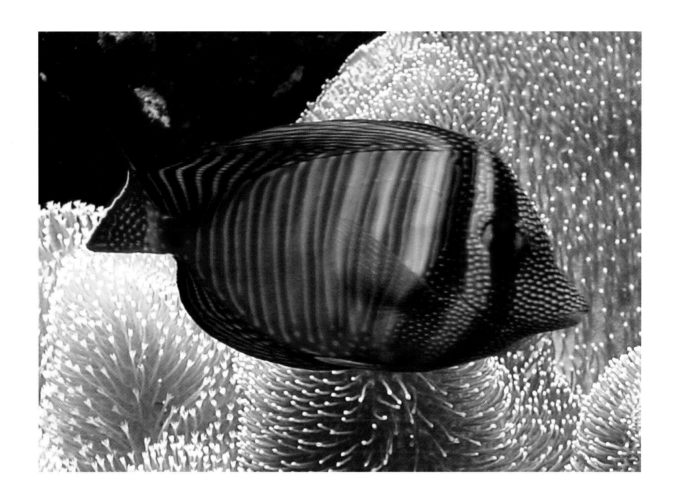

Zebrasoma desjardini (Red Sea Salfin Tang)

❏ **Origin:** Red Sea.
❏ **Captive Behavior:** An easy fish to keep; feeds on bubble algae (*Valonia* sp.) sometimes.

Acanthurus leucosternon (Powder Blue Tang)

❏ **Origin:** Maldives.
❏ **Captive Behavior:** Prone to parasite infections, a difficult fish to acclimate.

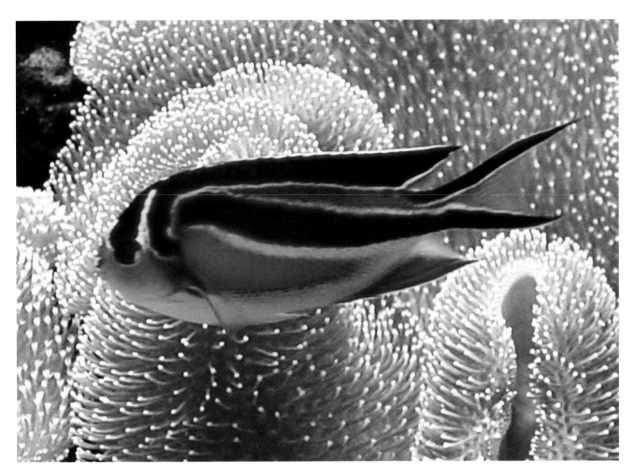

Genicanthus bellus (female)

❏ **Origin:** Western Pacific.
❏ **Captive Behavior:** A rare but hardy species.

Pygoplites diacanthus (Regal Angel)

❏ **Origin:** Red Sea.
❏ **Captive Behavior:** Shy, difficult to feed initially. Can do just fine once it settles down.

Opposite above & below:
The ***Pygoplites diacanthus*** (Regal Angel) is a highly desirable fish for many marine aquarists because of
 its striking color, but only those from the Red Sea have a good survival rate in captivity.

The anemone fishes often spawn in captive reef aquaria if proper conditions are provided.

Opposite above:
A pair of Percula Clownfish (***Amphiprion ocellaris***) just laid
orange eggs at the base of their host anemone.
Opposite below:
It takes as little as seven days for those orange eggs
to develop into un-hatched larvae with silver eyes.

The Maroon Clownfish (*Premnas biaculeatus*) is a very aggressive species.

This pair of Maroon Clown (*Premnas biaculeatus*) traveled all the way across the tank to harass their tankmate.

Marine Fish Breeding

Today, many marine fishes successfully reproduce in captivity. There are large numbers of commercial breeding programs that raise marine fish for aquarium hobbyist throughout the world. In South Asia, 16 species of marine fish are currently being raised, including the Blue-lined angel (*Chaetodontoplus septentrionalis*) and the Maculosus angel (*Pomacanthus maculosus*). The quality of these fishes is excellent. Because they were bred in captivity, they should adapt to our aquaria much easier than those caught in the wild.

Above:
A group of farm-raised juvenile Blue-lined angels (*Chaetodontoplus septentrionalis*).

Two-year-old farm raised adult Blue-lined angel (*Chaetodontoplus septentrionalis*).

A group of farm-raised juvenile Maculosus angels (*Pomacanthus maculosus*).

Coral Propagation

As collecting of marine life from coral reefs becomes more difficult or prohibited in the future, this hobby might have to rely on our ability to raise and culture these colorful corals that we all enjoy.

During the past several years, large numbers of coral fragments have been given out from my own system, and I have seen the second and third generations already.

The following pages show how easily soft and stony corals can be propagated in home aquaria.

The overgrowing branch can be trimmed with a pair of pliers.

The cut fragments are mounted to a small piece of rock with underwater epoxy.

If ideal conditions are provided, the new growth will soon cover the epoxy.

Opposite above:
A branch has just been trimmed.
Opposite below:
The new growth can be seen in as little as two weeks.

A fragment was mounted by using the gel-type crazy glue. This method has to be done outside the aquarium.

Opposite above & below:
Mounted fragments in the coral production/holding tank.

This leather coral (*Sarcophyton* **sp**.) has grown too large; it has started to shade the *Motipora digitata* and clam that are on each side.

A small piece of rock was placed near its base (*left*). It will take a couple of weeks for this rock to attach, then it can be trimmed by using a pair of sharp scissors (*right*).

It can now be safely moved to another aquarium. (***above***)

A soft coral of this size can release a large amount of slime when disturbed. If it is trimmed before attached to a piece of rock, it will be difficult to make it stay because of the strong water current in our reef system. Trying to tie it with rubber bands or string could cause infection or damage.

The same technique can also be applied to other soft corals such as colt coral (*Alcyonium* sp.), star polyps (*Briareum* sp.), *Xenia* sp., and mushroom anemone.

A small piece of rock was placed near the base of this green *Sinularia* sp. prior to the trimming.

Once the piece of rock is attached to the body, it is ready to be trimmed.

It becomes two separate pieces.

Soft corals can reproduce by splitting their bodies. The above picture shows a small piece of this Leather coral (*Sarcophyton* sp.) that is about to separate.

Opposite above:
Rubber bands are most suitable to temporarily hold a small piece like this and they can be removed as soon as it is attached.
Opposite below:
A few weeks later, it grows into a nice small colony.

A coral farming project that Daniel Knop has initiated in the island of Sambangan in central Java, Indonesia.

Photo: Daniel Knop

Corals are being fragmented, mounted on substrate, and attached to sheets made out of bamboo.

They mainly grow in cement frames in the sea (*above*), but they can also be transferred to and grown in land-based tanks (*opposite*).

Photo: Daniel Knop

Photographic Details

Cameras:
35 mm Leica R5 with 60 mm Macro-Elmarit-R f/2.8 and 90 mm Summicron-R f/2 lenses.
120 mm Bronica SQ with 80 mm f/4 lens and 2X converter.
4.1 Mega Pixels Sony DSC-S85 digital still camera with Carl Zeiss Vario-Sonnar 2/7-21 lens.

Images:
Kodak 200, 400, and 800 ASA films were used. Sets of color transparency were produced when film was processed.
Images are stored onto Kodak Photo CD format for web and publications.

Scanner:
Nikon Super CoolScan 4000 ED film/slide scanner.

A marine aquarium is enjoyable everyday,

but caring for it is never finished.

About the Author

Wayne Shang began keeping marine aquaria in the early 1980s after keeping freshwater fish since childhood. In the past ten years, he has focused on keeping small poly stony corals and *Tridacna* clams. Pictures of his aquariums have appeared in numerous books, magazines, and on the Internet.

Wayne holds a MBA degree from Concordia University. He is also a Ph.D. candidate in global business management. Although keeping marine life is his hobby, he has contributed his experience to overseas commercial breeding programs which raise marine fish and clams. He also takes time from his busy schedule to speak at local aquarium societies and clubs to share his knowledge and help other aquarists solve their problems.

Wayne currently maintains a 700-gallon reef aquarium and a 300-gallon marine fish-only aquarium at his residence in California.